TICKS

by Patrick Merrick

The Child's World

Content Adviser:
Jeffrey Hahn,
Department of Entomology,
University of Minnesota

Published in the United States of America by The Child's World®
PO Box 326 • Chanhassen, MN 55317-0326
800-599-READ • www.childsworld.com

PHOTO CREDITS

© Anthony Bannister; Gallo Images/Corbis: cover, 1, 9
© Arco Images/Alamy: 27
© Blickwinkel/Alamy: 12, 13
© CDC/PHIL/Corbis: 7
© Imagebroker/Alamy: 5
© James Zipp/Photo Researchers, Inc., 25
© Kevin Schafer/Corbis: 11
© Larry Mulvehill/Photo Researchers, Inc.: 23 (top)
© Nigel J. Dennis/Photo Researchers, Inc.: 21
© Robert Noonan/Photo Researchers, Inc.: 28
© Roger De La Harpe/Gallo Images/Corbis: 19
© Scott Camazine/Photo Researchers, Inc.: 17, 23 (bottom)
© Troy Bartlett/Alamy: 8
© Wim van Egmond/Visuals Unlimited: 15

ACKNOWLEDGMENTS

The Child's World®: Mary Berendes, Publishing Director;
Katherine Stevenson, Editor

The Design Lab: Kathleen Petelinsek, Design and Page Production

LIBRARY OF CONGRESS CATALOGING-IN-PUBLICATION DATA

Merrick, Patrick.
  Ticks / by Patrick Merrick.
     p. cm. — (New naturebooks)
  Includes bibliographical references and index.
  ISBN 1-59296-651-9 (library bound : alk. paper)
  1. Ticks—Juvenile literature. I. Title. II. Series.
  QL458.M54 2006
  595.4'29—dc22   2006001378

Table of Contents

On the cover: Bont ticks like this one are common in South Africa.

Meet the Tick!

Ticks have been around for about 90 million years—since the time of the dinosaurs! The oldest tick found so far is called *Carios jerseyi*. It was discovered in New Jersey.

It's a warm spring day, and you're hiking in a park. You follow a path along the edge of a meadow. Soft grasses brush against your pants legs with every step. You hike all afternoon, enjoying the sun and the outdoors. When you get home, you feel something tickling the back of your knee. You take a look and find a small, flat brown bug walking slowly across your skin. It's a good thing you found it—if you hadn't, it would have attached itself to your skin and sucked your blood! What is this pesky little bug? It's a tick!

After a short walk in the woods, you might see ticks like this one crawling on your skin or clothing.

What Are Ticks?

An arachnid's cephalothorax holds its sense organs and its mouthparts. All four pairs of legs attach to it, too.

Ticks look a lot like other summertime bugs, but they are actually very different. Most bugs are **insects**. Insects have six legs and a pair of feelers, or **antennae**. They have three main parts to their bodies—a head, a middle part (called the **thorax**), and a back end (called the **abdomen**). Insects usually have wings, too.

Ticks belong to a different animal group called **arachnids**. Spiders, scorpions, and mites are arachnids, too. Arachnids have eight legs instead of six. Their bodies have two main parts instead of three. Their back end is still called an abdomen. But their head and middle section are combined into one part called a *cephalothorax* (seh-fuh-luh-THOR-aks). Arachnids don't have antennae, and they don't have wings.

6

Black-legged ticks like this one are also called deer ticks. They are found in many parts of North America.

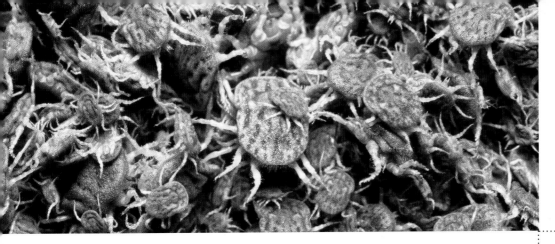

Tampan ticks are a type of soft tick. You can see how their bodies are different from the hard tick on page 8. Tampan ticks feed mostly on birds.

There are about 850 different kinds, or **species**, of ticks in the world. Ticks come in gray, brown, black, red, or off-white colors. Some are a combination of colors, and some have patterns on them. Ticks' coloring can make them hard to see in the outdoors. Some ticks are as small as a tiny dot. Others are up to an inch (2.5 cm) long.

Scientists divide ticks into two main families. *Hard ticks* are flatter and have a hard covering called a *scutum* that protects most of their body. Hard ticks have mouthparts you can see from above, and the male and female ticks look different. *Soft ticks* are rounder and don't have a scutum. Their mouthparts are tucked away underneath their bodies and can't be seen from above. Male and female soft ticks look very similar.

There's a third family of ticks, but it has only one species—*Nuttalliella namaqua*, found only in parts of Africa. This species has features of both hard and soft ticks.

Female hard ticks have a smaller scutum than the males. This allows females' bodies to grow much larger when they feed on blood. They need the extra blood for laying eggs.

American dog ticks like this one got their name because they are often found on dogs in the United States.

What Do Ticks Eat?

Some soft ticks can live for years without eating.

Ticks often climb up plants and wait for a host to pass by. An animal must be very close for ticks to climb aboard, because ticks can't jump or fly.

Ticks eat only one thing—blood! They are **parasites** that live and feed on other animals, called their *hosts*.

Soft ticks and hard ticks eat differently. When a soft tick finds a host, it waits in the host's nest to feed. A soft tick might feed for only a few minutes and then hide again in the nest. When a hard tick feeds from a host, it stays attached the entire time, until it is filled with blood.

Ticks find an animal by sensing movement, heat, or the animal's breath. If the tick is close enough, it grabs onto the animal's fur, feathers, or skin. Tiny claws on its legs help it cling. Ticks can crawl and climb quite well.

Several ticks are feeding on this toad. Can you tell which one has been feeding the longest?

palps

hypostome
chelicerae (inside hypostome)

This picture shows a female sheep tick after a huge meal of blood. She is resting near a matchstick. Sheep ticks are also called pasture ticks. They are common in Europe.

A tick has mouthparts specially made for feeding on blood. The outer mouthparts look like pinchers, but they're really *palps* used for feeling, tasting, and smelling. The tick's *chelicerae* (kih-LIH-ser-ee) cut through the host's skin to get to the animal's blood. The tick uses its straw-like *hypostome* to drink the blood.

A tick's body is designed to hold lots of blood. As the tick feeds, its abdomen grows. Soft ticks can gain up to 10 times their body weight when they feed. Hard ticks can gain as much as 600 times their body weight!

If you were a tick the same size you are now (say, 66 pounds or 30 kg), how much would you weigh after a big meal of blood? If you were a soft tick, you might weigh up to 660 pounds (200 kg). If you were a hard tick, you might weight up to 39,600 pounds (18,000 kg)!

This close-up photo of a sheep tick shows the tick's mouthparts. On the hypostome, you can see the tiny, backward-pointing hooks, or barbs, that help keep the tick from being pulled off its host. Many hard ticks also produce a substance that makes a hard "plug" between their mouthparts and the host's skin. The "plug" keeps the tick attached.

13

What Are Baby Ticks Like?

Hard-tick adults usually die after mating and laying eggs. Soft ticks can mate and lay eggs several times before they die.

A tick larva can wait for quite a while—even two or three months—before finding a host.

Adult ticks mate after they feed. The females quickly lay their eggs—up to 3,000 of them. They lay them on plants, in dead leaves, or on the ground.

When the eggs hatch, they produce baby ticks, called **larvae**. The larvae have only six legs, rather than eight like the adults. For a larva to move into the next stage of its life, it must fill up on blood and go through some big changes. First, it finds a host animal and begins to feed.

This close-up picture shows a sheep tick larva. Newly hatched ticks are often called "seed ticks" because they look like tiny seeds.

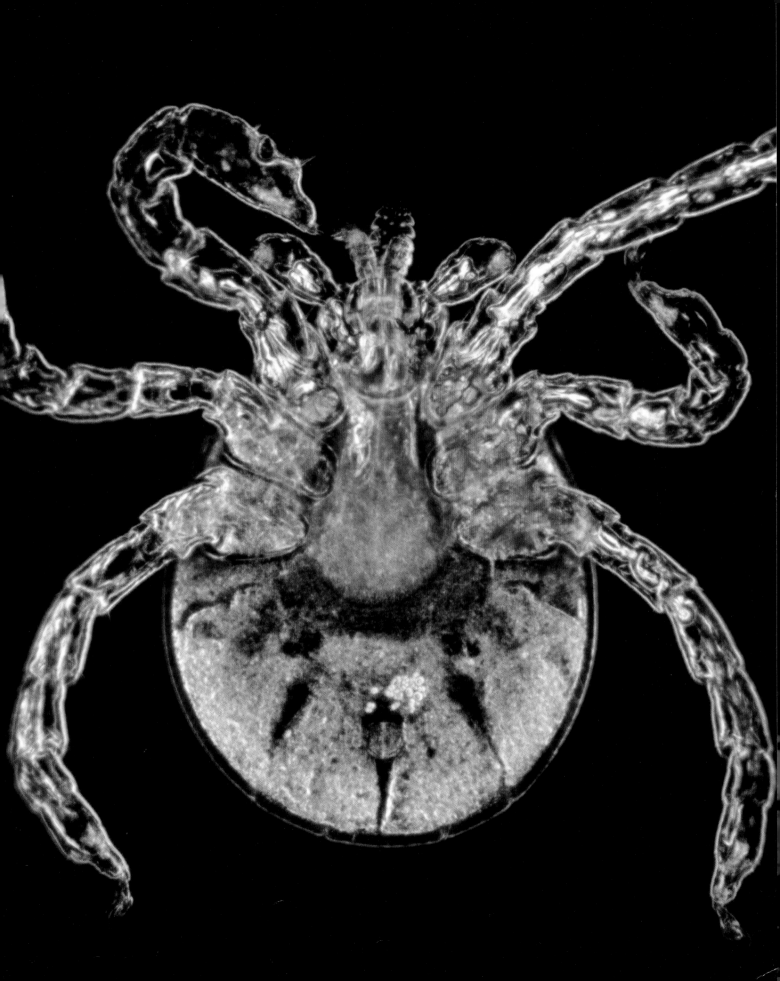

When a larva has had enough blood, it drops off the host and finds a safe place to shed its skin, or **molt**. Under the old skin is a bigger baby tick. In this next stage of its life, the tick is called a **nymph**.

The nymph finds a new animal host and starts feeding again. It must molt at least one more time before it becomes an adult. When the nymph has had enough blood and is ready, it again drops off the host and molts. This time, it becomes an adult.

A hard tick eats only three times in its entire life—once as a larva, once as a nymph, and once as an adult. Soft ticks eat more often.

Some hard ticks have the same type of host for their whole life, while others have as many as three.

A soft-tick larva or nymph might feed several times before it molts. A hard-tick larva or nymph stays attached until it is filled with enough blood to molt.

Here you can see three black-legged (deer) ticks. The smallest one is a nymph, the medium-sized one is an adult male, and the largest one is an adult female.

17

Where Do Ticks Live?

Black-legged (deer) ticks dry out easily, so they aren't as common in drier areas. American dog ticks, on the other hand, can survive well in areas with less moisture.

Brown dog ticks are one of the few kinds that can become serious pests inside people's homes.

Ticks of one kind or another live all over the world—wherever there are host animals on which they can feed. They live in deserts, forests, and grasslands, and even in the Arctic and Antarctic.

Ticks live throughout the United States and Canada. They are especially common in places with lots of tall grass, weeds, bushes, and piles of dead grass and leaves. Ticks normally live outdoors. Sometimes, though, they fasten themselves to people or pets and end up in people's homes. They don't usually last very long indoors.

These colorful bont ticks are feeding on a rhinoceros in South Africa. Bont ticks are common in Africa and the Caribbean and often feed on livestock.

Do Any Animals Eat Ticks?

Some types of ticks feed on chickens, but chickens feed on ticks, too! People sometimes keep flocks of chickens or guinea fowl to help control ticks.

In one study, scientists looked at the stomach contents of 53 oxpeckers and reported finding 22,000 ticks!

Ticks seem as though they wouldn't have many enemies, but quite a few animals eat them. The best known are African birds called red-billed and yellow-billed oxpeckers, also called tickbirds. Oxpeckers ride around on rhinos, cattle, and other large animals, eating blood-filled ticks. Like the ticks, however, the oxpeckers are also parasites. They pick at sores or wounds and feed on the animals' blood.

Shrews and some other small animals eat ticks, and so do spiders and some insects, including fire ants. Some wasps lay their eggs on tick larvae. When the eggs hatch, the wasp larvae feed on the young ticks and kill them. In some areas, people have tried introducing these wasps to reduce the number of ticks.

20

These four oxpeckers are keeping this impala's back free of ticks and other parasites.

Are Ticks Dangerous?

Rocky Mountain spotted fever and Lyme disease were both named for the places where they were first reported— the Rocky Mountains, and the town of Lyme, Connecticut.

Lyme disease is usually spread to humans by tick nymphs. The nymphs are so tiny, people often don't even notice them.

Most tick bites aren't serious, but some ticks carry germs that cause disease. In many parts of the world, tick-spread diseases are a big problem. Ticks pick up the germs from animals they bite, then pass them along when they bite other animals. In North America, the best-known tick-spread diseases are Rocky Mountain spotted fever and Lyme disease.

Rocky Mountain spotted fever is spread most often by American dog ticks and Rocky Mountain wood ticks. It's less common than Lyme disease but more serious—it can even cause death, especially if it isn't treated quickly.

Lyme disease rarely kills people, but it can cause serious problems, from achy and swollen joints to muscle, nerve, and heart problems. It's spread by black-legged (deer) ticks and western black-legged ticks.

Top photo: If you see this type of bull's-eye rash on your body, get to a doctor right away. A rash in this shape can be a sign of Lyme disease.

Bottom photo: Black-legged (deer) ticks are tiny. The one next to this paper clip is an adult!

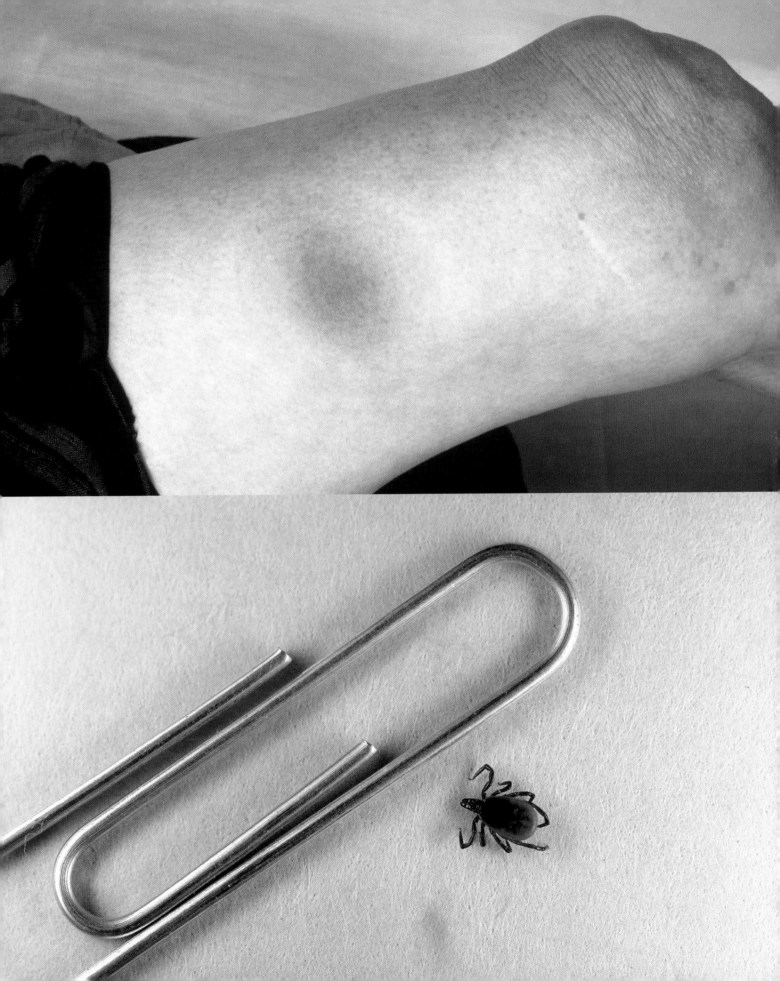

How Can You Protect Yourself from Ticks?

Find out what kinds of ticks live in your area, what kinds of diseases they carry, and when they're most active. Doctors, nature centers, and libraries often have this information available or can tell you where to find it.

If you are going to a place where ticks are likely, make it hard for the ticks to get to your skin! Long pants and a long-sleeved shirt can help. So can tucking your pants legs into your boots or pulling them down over high boots. Putting bug spray on your clothes can help, too—but be sure it's a clothing spray that's specially made for keeping ticks away! Put long hair in a pony tail, and don't sit on the ground.

Check your clothes, skin, and hair for ticks while you are still outside. That way they can't come into your house with you! If your pets were outside with you, check them, too.

When you get inside, check yourself carefully. Ticks especially like to crawl into hidden areas, such as under your arms or in your hair, or where your clothing presses against you.

Many parks and walking trails have signs like this, to help you remember to protect yourself from ticks.

ALERT

Actual size

Deer ticks inhabiting this area may carry Lyme Disease. Remove ticks from body and clothing.

What Should You Do If You Get a Tick Bite?

Old ways of removing ticks included burning them with a match, squeezing them, or coating them with something. These ways aren't safe, and they almost never work. They can actually make the tick pass germs into your body! You shouldn't touch ticks with your bare hands, either.

If you find a tick on you, stay calm! Even when a tick is attached, it takes a while for it to pass on any diseases—and most ticks aren't disease-carriers anyway. But you should remove the tick as soon as possible.

To remove it, you should have an adult's help, and you'll need to know how to do it correctly. Have your parents call your doctor or talk to your school nurse to find out how. You might be told to save the tick, in case you get sick from the bite.

Things to watch out for include skin rashes, headaches, fever, swollen joints, an upset stomach, or feeling sore or tired. If you notice a problem where you were bitten, or if you get sick (even if it's a few weeks later), tell your doctor right away. But chances are, you'll be fine!

Just as with people, the best way to remove ticks from pets is with tweezers. Always be sure an adult helps you, even when you're removing ticks from your pets.

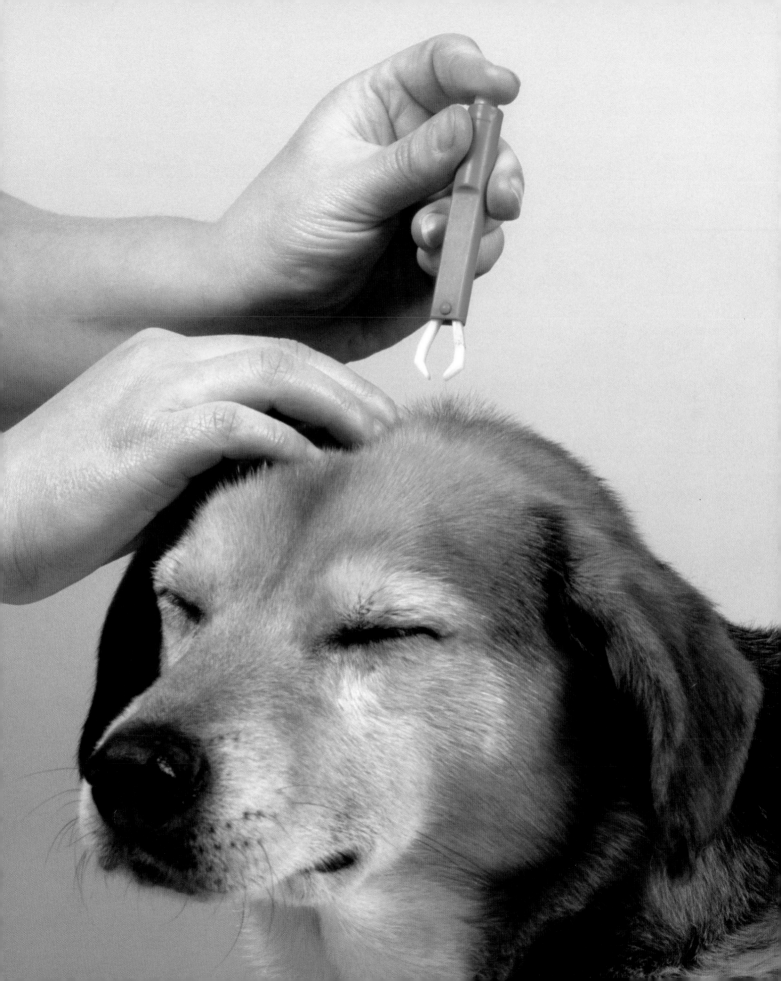

Some people are scared of ticks because they think tick bites will hurt them. Many people find ticks disgusting because they suck blood. The truth is, ticks suck blood for the same reason you eat a sandwich—because it's good for them and helps them grow. Ticks might seem like pests, but they're also a part of the natural world, and they've been around for a very, very long time. Ticks can be a problem, but if you take the right steps to be careful around them, there's no reason to let them stop you from enjoying the outdoors!

Ticks usually have to be attached to someone for at least 24 to 36 hours before they can pass on diseases.

This lone star tick is "questing" at the top of a blade of grass. Ticks stand in this position when they are seeking a new host. They hold two or four legs out from their bodies, ready to grab on to a passing animal's skin or fur. Lone star ticks are named for the white dot on the female's back.

Glossary

abdomen (AB-duh-men) On insects and some other animals, the abdomen is the entire rear section of the body. A tick's abdomen swells when it feeds.

antennae (an-TEH-nee) Antennae are movable feelers on the heads of insects and some other animals that help them find out about their surroundings. Ticks and other arachnids don't have any antennae.

arachnids (uh-RAK-nidz) Arachnids are boneless animals that have eight legs, two main body parts (a cephalothorax and an abdomen), and no wings. Ticks are arachnids.

insects (IN-sekts) Insects are boneless animals that have six legs, three main body parts (a head, a thorax, and an abdomen), and usually one or two pairs of wings. Ticks are not insects.

larvae (LAR-vee) In some animals, larvae are the young, very different forms of the animals when they first hatch or are born. The larvae go through big changes before they become adults.

molt (MOLT) To molt is to get rid of an old, outer layer of skin, shell, hair, or feathers. As tick nymphs grow, they molt several times.

nymph (NIMF) "Nymph" is the name for certain baby insects (or arachnids) that go through some changes in form, but not a complete change, before they become adults.

parasites (PAYR-uh-syts) Parasites are plants or animals that live on or inside other living things, feeding off of them. Ticks are parasites.

species (SPEE-sheez) An animal species is a group of animals that share the same features and can have babies only with animals in the same group. There are about 850 different species of ticks.

thorax (THOR-aks) An insect's thorax is the middle part of its body. Ticks are not insects, so they do not have a thorax.

To Find Out More

Read It!

Hirschmann, Kris. *Ticks.* San Diego, CA: Kidhaven Press, 2004.

Sill, Catherine P., and John Sill (illustrator). *About Arachnids: A Guide for Children.* Atlanta, GA: Peachtree, 2003.

Silverstein, Alvin, Virginia B. Silverstein, and Laura Silverstein Nunn. *Lyme Disease.* Danbury, CT: Franklin Watts, 2000.

On the Web

Visit our home page for lots of links about ticks:
http://www.childsworld.com/links

Note to Parents, Teachers, and Librarians: We routinely check our Web links to make sure they're safe, active sites—so encourage your readers to check them out!

31

Index

About the Author

When Pat Merrick was a child, his family traveled and moved many times. He became fascinated with science and finding out about the world around him. In college he majored in science and education. After college, Mr. Merrick and his wife both decided to become teachers and try and help kids learn to love the world around them. He has taught science to all levels of kids, from kindergarten through twelfth grade. When not teaching or writing, Mr. Merrick loves to read and play with his six children. Pat Merrick currently lives in a small town in southern Minnesota with his wife and family.